THE GREAT BOOK OF
Cryptograms

Louise B. Moll

Illustrated by Jim Sharpe

Sterling Publishing Co., Inc. New York

For Harold
Being deeply loved by someone gives you strength,
While loving someone deeply gives you courage.

Lao Tzu

Acknowledgment
I thank my son-in-law, Dr. Jan Tobochnik, for
writing the computer program that produced the
cryptograms.

Library of Congress Cataloging-in-Publication Data

Moll, Louise B.
    Great book of cryptograms / Louise B. Moll : illustrated by Jim
Sharpe.
        p.   cm.
    Includes index.
    ISBN 0-8069-8784-7
    1. Cryptograms. I. Title.
GV1507.C8M65 1993
793.73—dc20   92-39447
                                             CIP

10 9 8 7 6

Published by Sterling Publishing Company, Inc.
387 Park Avenue South, New York, N.Y. 10016
© 1993 by Louise B. Moll
Illustrations © 1993 by Jim Sharpe
Distributed in Canada by Sterling Publishing
℅ Canadian Manda Group, P.O.Box 920, Station U
Toronto, Ontario, Canada M8Z 5P9
Distributed in Great Britain and Europe by Cassell PLC
Villiers House, 41/47 Strand, London WC2N 5JE, England
Distributed in Australia by Capricorn Link Ltd.
P.O. Box 665, Lane Cove, NSW 2066
Manufactured in the United States of America

Sterling ISBN 0-8069-8784-7

Contents

A Note for Cryptographers

If you're a cryptogram lover, you'll know how difficult it has been to find any cryptogram collections. You solve the handful in the crossword puzzle magazines, of course, but then what? The buffs who want to settle into a cozy, long evening with pencil, eraser and enough cryptograms to last the night, are out of luck.

Finding no books available in stores or racks anywhere, I decided to put one together myself. Since it is important to find a meaningful message when you break a code, I began searching through philosophy books. What better source of material could there be than the greatest sages of all time!

The quotations in this book span the centuries and are as significant today as they were when they were written. For me, they open doors in my mind and provide food for my soul. I hope you get as much pleasure from solving them as I had in selecting and disguising them.

How to Use This Book

A cryptogram is a communication in code, using a scrambled alphabet that substitutes one letter for another. Breaking it is an exercise in logic, imagination and perseverance. Logic, as you search out the patterns and structure of the words and sentences you're trying to uncover. Imagination, as you intuit words from the jumble before you. Perseverance, as you stick with the trial and error search.

If you've never solved a cryptogram before, you'll need to know certain facts: Each cryptogram is coded differently, but in any single quotation, the code is consistent. No letter ever stands for itself.

For example, a C could represent an E throughout the message, and an F could be an R.

WE'RE PUZZLED PUZZLERS
HC'FC KYNNACP KYNNACFX

The most common three–letter words include *the, and, but, for* and *are*. Common two–letter words are *it, is, of*, and *in*. Long word endings include *ing, ion, est* and *ied*.

Start by tracking down these telltale patterns, and with the letters you detect, you'll soon clue into other formations that will eventually reveal the message.

The order of frequency of the most used letters in the English language is:

E–T–A–0–I–N–S–H–R–D–L–U

And it has probably never helped anyone to know that!
Have fun with these crypts!

Aesop
(6th Century B.C.)

1. 'BLH OSST MTCLNF BS ASSW PFGSVF QF AFME.

2. 'AHR AKO SFZA VY F QHRO WFP AV SZOYOZ AKHPMR POUORRFZX GOYVZO WFAAOZR VY UJZHVRHAX, VZPFWOPA VZ SNOFRJZO.

3. HNQKUWO JPAUZB QW NLFP, WNPO BQO; QZX FLBW GPLGSP QKP TUZX WL WNPUK ZPUANJLKB CLK WNPUK LYZ BQTPB.

4. TMAYSQA VSSC PIAQFU IPC VFIAMAQCU, DUP YIC IW VSSC NMZU MP I TMNCUFPUWW IW MP I WSJMUAG.

5. JAMBKR BW MVI UHWBRIWW KP GBPI, JRS MVILI'W RK MVKHNVM KP IFIL AKEBRN MK MVI IRS KP KHL OKHLRIQ BR MBEI BP XI WGIIZ UQ MVI XJQ.

6. ZTVUV OUV AE LAOUVL LE XOAIVUEPL OL ZTELV ZTOZ OUV JONX HEU PL PAXVU ZTV AOQV EH IEEX EHHNDVL.

7. AWL BAATYDV PAZE YD LWAKCV IA DRAYT J CAAE FJKDL, JWE 'IYD UJWX J UJW'D BAZIKWL IA FKI VYD APW IVZAJI PYIV VYD APW JZCKULWID.

8. LY LZ GNNWDJLPT YW SDOJAPNA, GZ MAUU GZ PGYODA, YW SGF YRGY RWPWD YW FWOD SGDAPYZ, YRGY FWO AVSANY FWOD NRLUJDAP ZRWOUJ SGF YW FWO.

9. SGR KV NUK TGAHUWZ WK UTYGZAWRF, KVZ HZGAPNG WK HZVAHGZWRF, MVZ USS RLWKIA UZG BLUKIGUESG.

10. LOMNG EST MGQ SBBSTMVUFMFQY
SE PSFUJ MGFUJY, EST MGQTQ'Y
USMGFUJ LQII PSUQ HVM LGOM'Y
PSUQ FU YQOYSU.

Answers on page 102.

Aristotle

(384–322 B.C.)

1. GLYHH MTNG DV QDDW VDPNFXK DP DV TNG DAADGTNK JHKYPHB WD XDN KVVKJN NCK MYHYXJK DV HTVK DX DXK GTWK DP NCK DNCKP.

2. USG JEJLQGNCUW GNIG CD ECDCKAJ ZJOJUZD FOSU ACWNG BSL CGD ECDCKCACGQ.

3. EW QIT DSMF ED OSKTY, QIT OSDQ ZXSGPGFT KETR ED QIPQ RIPQ OSKTD EQ ED DTUDEGFT QIEUCD.

4. KWRRAVSGG AG FHHO WMBACABI, VHB WEZGSESVB.

5. LRP MDNPEDP WC LRP UWWH CWA OGE NM YWJNLNDM.

6. EKUFAW FH LKJX KP DQX XHHXABX KP PJFXAOHQFY DQIA MXFAW EKUXO.

7. VY ETL SP HTVB YJTY PAPNL
VXBVAVBMTF ETX, TXB TFF EPX VX
WIEEIX, TVE TY T WPNYTVX PXB
KJVWJ BPYPNEVXPH KJTY YJPL WJIIHP
TXB KJTY YJPL TAIVB.

8. EYZYJ TP UEA UYHAZ YS N BNZ'P
VATZX SNBYQP SYJ OYTZX XYYO.

9. VMJKBS YJFNMC PNBR BRM BNHM
ZO INOM.

10. LGH HBF DBF LGH PHDBE LAZDIFE
NL PDV YAPH DCAQL CV YGDBYH.

Answers on pages 102–103.

St. Augustine

(354–430)

1. GR G LGOBDQ UR G DUITS UO STQ OUITS, RM STQ FVRS HGO UR G DUITS UO STQ BGPEOQRR MY STUR CMPDB.

2. VUEZXS AWJFPWE, APW EXQR CWBWDAE, APW GRWEP EPWZE AWJCE.

3. IX GQDU AP ISK CQUAPSRKUI XM ISK ZAYOKV, IX WAFK HAWSI AP ISK SNCCAUKPP XM ISK LQPI.

4. ALF BFYVF QZ YMM ALHSPX HX ALF AEYSUTHMMHAC QZ QEGFE.

5. CB CV TYB BPH GYLI, GAB BPH FYEEAKBCGCNCBI YJ BPH GYLI, BPQB CV GAELHTVYRH BY BPH VYAN.

6. TND OJ COLTE DWUNDANY WOY VLDLNJ WR SZLDA ZRE TWQN, ZRE DANX KLTT CN LRQLRVLCTN.

7. LNLAP ZTC VLLHV WLTQL JP
KTDRCD KTA, JFM CG ZTC VLLHV KTA
JP ZTHRCD WLTQL.

8. KCGPECB DN PEC SJDLZXLW KXB
DN PEC RGHGZ PECXZXAN UXCW JKN
XKC XDPJGK CPCBKJZ ZGSC.

9. SZ TFUR SZ LFB HBJIDU LFBJ
WDSJK XNKW KWNURZ FQ DSJKW, SJD
LFB UFK EFBJKNUR WDSANUDZZ FQ
WDSJK?

10. CJOK, XJW HAO MOBCFLOM CW
MFO, LOOM LWC YO PHAOSZQ CW
FLUZFAO XJHC MOHCJ CJOK HAO CW
MFO, YZC FLCW XJHC RQHPO MOHCJ
XFQQ ZBJOA CJOG.

Answers on pages 103–104.

Francis Bacon

(1561–1626)

1. C TCX QKCQ JA HUEXM JX HNCPA,
TCH VN UYB JX KUEPA, JL KN KCA
YUAQ XU QJTN.

2. NYXKZ LMK OASUD BKU'Z
BYZCMKZZKZ, HABWLUYAUZ GAM
BYVVJK LDK, LUV AJV BKU'Z USMZKZ.

3. HPO JGOLHOMH HGNMH, COHZOOT
QLT LTE QLT, KM HPO HGNMH RI
JKWKTJ YRNTMOF.

4. OAUEU NL LGEUZV XF KEUBOUE
YNLPFW, OABX YUZZ OF ONWU OAU
RUKNXXNXK, BXP FXLUO FQ OANXKL.

5. PRAJHY ZPH WKP YVHQERQD; ZQE
YVHQERQD WKP JKQKP ZQE DKKE
ZASRKQY.

6. E LZYYTM LZKK HELWRV DRMMRH
MWZY MWR DZOOZOR TB JEHMIR.

7. HJBDMF DM LOF JFVGFXLDWU WV TDJLQF.

8. CDQ FLZZLZM EG DEZEN LV YOC CDQ NQWQRKLZM EG R HRZ'V WLNCOQ RZJ FENCD, FLCDEOC JLVRJWRZCRMQ.

9. XFGQJPJE FGA WJJI CEUPJN WB GZQFUERQRJA RA NJQJEYRIJN JPJI YUEJ HJEQGRIKB TEUY QFJ JDCJERJIHJ UT GIB YGI.

10. NOJ IKH EX BKCZKNQEP QB EPJ, KCNOEYRO NOJVJ AKH FJ AKPH BNJGB; FYN IQBTEA QB NOJ IKH NE BKCZKNQEP.

Answers on pages 104–105.

Martin Buber

(1878–1965)

1. HFYW VE NJPT MFY NJS, SFI NJS MFY HFYW.

2. OMB OKBB SV UTVB RDI IBYBK LB XTZPSTIOBX VKSF OMB OKBB SV AISQUBXNB VSK LSOM MDYB SIB DIX OMB ZDFB KSSO.

3. RQPK JROMEMTY MV Q KTFVR TS HKR KFUQY VTFO OTYEMYE STJ ETG.

4. T JYKGBDN VYE MDAKGW TGDV VKJYEQJ CTNKGA JE MDAKG TGDV KG TFF DTNGDWJ LQWJ RTKF.

5. NM RUYC NM KNY DQFOQBEQM HPQ MQRX NM NY UATQOH, PQ BM YUH SYBHQV.

6. KVBFU BN FUH QBJFTOBTYN VME FOBYXCUVMF XHNNVSH.

7. IOM LYMTI KMTQM CZ ZPSMIOCVL MZZMVICTJJB WCEEMYMVI EYPS IOM TAZMVQM PE GTY.

8. RIXYT GDQW RFHY WGE RHDY YG SGLLEDXSHYT; RIXYT VG YFHY XY XV SGLLEDXSHYTP.

9. HZI OTWKU WCNTXM WN BK WKQTIWCBKDT MIHA HZI MHITOTBIN CQBC PT OTVZTBCQ CH HZI DQWXEITK.

10. PZC EAVWN AG FJY ERPZABP PZC HABW AG RP RY JNNRPRAY RH YA ZBFJY EAVWN; XBP JWHA PZC HABW AG FJY ERPZABP PZC EAVWN RY JNNRPRAY RH YA ZBFJY HABW.

Answers on pages 105–106.

Buddha
(Siddhartha Gautama)
(563–483 B.C.)

1. NBMMNH LO NBMMNH XGKM MDH XBTAK WI XHT LH MQJBTHA IWQ DBVDHQ MQGMDK.

2. RQ RXX FRHMNFC GFQQFXQ JRZF LK MNF SAMMFH FCZ BC LFBCD LHAVFC, QA BQ MNF XBIF AI JAHMRXQ.

3. ZPACH RPA OJSN ZA JCUSVH OAV ZPH ZVFZP PJXH DSCCHE ZPH UFVUACH AO NSOH.

4. MXKMO JF MOY YFFYPQY DG RJGY, GDX MXKMO YPCKXYMO LYBDPC MOY CYVMO DG MOY LDCB.

5. V QTYG OVY KAR OVQUM CRRG JMU RH ATM KUVENA TM FTCANEI MVTG NR SRMMUMM V CFUVN NFUVMJFU; LJN NAU OTMUF KAR ARVFGM JS ATM FTZAUM KTEE AVPU YR SFRHTN.

6. BSUDVP PCSU GNZUFY ZKM JNZYN FC EDAA; FGZF DY FUSN UNADXDCK.

7. GMJSMKC GMDKM KDB HEMYY QBYT EIMJM DYY XDBUCT IDR HURDGGMDJMH.

8. DEB MDDA DB PYJI APPAR ODIIDZ ER UDQFJQEKIIT IJWP RXKADZR.

9. JGBIFX RP FRMRAO KBICVGBIJ JCY VUI BIJGFVJ TP CFF VUIRB HIIHJ, VUIX YTGFH VGBA CYCX PBTD VUID RA HRJOGJV.

10. OETFT BN QP TLBI AKO ZEXO DIPZN DFPJ NTID.

Answers on page 106.

Samuel Clemens (Mark Twain)

(1835–1910)

1. JQNZK NQLZP FP HTXZKQNFTP SQPPTN CRKN QPIVTXI.

2. R TRB BXCXV VXRYPXF UPRU ZJSSI PXJAPU EO HJFZET HPXB PX YRB BE WEBAXV KX WXZ KI UPX BEFX.

3. BCOQGL UOH QLSXULC ASQXLC QIC HEDDLC QIC DICOTH—OROCX BCID XULHL WCOAMOGFH SX SH O BSQL GIEQXCK.

4. DXZ XG ZBP GNQQPM LRHHXROP FE XQPRG DBXSB VPEFHP ZBPXH NMXFM DPHP MFZ WPHSPXJPQ ZF BRJP RMI HPTRZXFM.

5. FK RCCZW LOS QLVSO; VICWS CX VIS HOSLV HSBNAWSW LOS QNBS. SUSOKRCJK JONBZW QLVSO.

6. RGGVYVGVTEV RX SMV EMHIDRBT
BO CRKVGSZ HTJ RSX BTCZ XLGV
JVOVTXV.

7. WSLK UKKDU FBK UYONFKUF, GAF
OF OU FBK UWSYKUF SN JWW
CZSYFBU.

8. YX JCB NIWSU GK NDITTKU ZYMF
MFK NCM YM ZIWSU YJHDIPK JCB,
GWM YM ZIWSU UKMKDYIDCMK MFK
NCM.

9. GV YBBGCFYVGN BYHSNFHZVJ FC
VZBZCCGKM JY PZZS XS YVZ'C
CZNT-KZCSZBJ.

10. ZL JPYLVLBB TO AXFY UYLBB TC
AXF EFBG, ZFG SLLQ P GTUA BXFV.

Answers on page 107.

Confucius

(551–479 B.C.)

1. WPJOPRK KYP YPMTPUEZ MUL PMWKYEZ JOAWAKJ MUL XPPO KYPV MK M LAJKMURP.

2. S KSE XOI OSH YIKKBGGVT S KBHGSWV SET TIVHE'G YICCVYG BG, BH YIKKBGGBEF SEIGOVC KBHGSWV.

3. J MFUSNFAJU KEFD UES WZJTDF J AJU EU SVF PJDTD EY XVJS VF DJQD, UEZ KEFD VF KFUQ SVF SZGSV EY XVJS EUF DJQD PFIJGDF VF KTDNTLFD SVF WFZDEU XVE DJQD TS.

4. XR TRJ GRFFO MARDJ YVRYUV TRJ PTRGWTL ORDF MAWUWJO, ADJ GRFFO JSMJ ORD SMHV TRJ LRJ WJ.

5. V NTQLGTHVQ JGVHTR AUHRTGX, SAUGT V EZHHZQ HVQ JGVHTR ZLATKR.

6. EG C SCU QKRPI ZM TMHMXM AKQCXI JESTMPG CUI WMUMXKRT AKQCXI KAJMXT, JM QKRPI UMHMX CXKRTM XMTMUASMUA.

7. G LGC QWF YFNT CFH HWACB GCY MIGC IFCE GWNGY QAII PACY HUFDJIN UAEWH JR WAT YFFU.

8. AMQOW HGDIDMYY KGFX HGDIDMYY, TRF AMQOW MCGU KGFX NRYFGJM.

9. AM AT JLP MFLM JLUGT MVCMF SVGLM, LPX PEM MVCMF MFLM JLUGT JLP SVGLM.

10. UYMR GBH BKNBHTG EYV MUSHTG QBEJEQGHJT VUY'G QBEYNH.

Answers on pages 107–108.

John Dewey

(1859–1952)

1. KFQ WDVQ LKVHSHRI KFQ WDVQ
TKKTHRWQRKL, UQVFTUL; AYK TJLD
TLLYVQGJC KFQ WDVQ RQQGL TRG
KFQ WDVQ GHLTUUDHRKWQRKL.

2. OBV XWZV TV GW QHG OBV XWZV
TV QDDWXJMCRB, OBV XWZV OBV VHG
CR LQHCOS QHG LVPQOCWH.

3. QCNARAMD AJ NPOK VKNTYVKV TM
PCO NPNKYMJ PI MOACNSQ MQTY TM
MQPJK PI ITARCOK.

4. CLSOLCIAMG MR IJAGKP BP IJLE
BSL AP HVI B PIBKL AG IJL CSMOLPP
MR QBXAGK IJLQ WARRLSLGI.

5. UQGXMMUBXQFX LXFCEXJ CPZJ UQ
GTX OXBZXX UQ YTUFT YX PJX UG
VQO VFFXAG ZXJACQJULUMUGN KCZ
FCQJXSPXQFXJ.

6. I TLSS ZIK BCONM LIQYSL QIFS YUA RYIKRS UK IK CHSK BCLNM QYIK VS JOILIKQSSM UK QYS RNCASM BCLNM.

7. EMSLEY LP GR YDYWYRH LR VOYYZSW GRZ HMYOY EGR IY RS EMSLEY QLHMSTH TROYGDLNYZ GRZ KOYEGOLSTP KSPPLILDLHLYP.

8. HPYSJBC SV ENYJ BWPR BWJ VGSAJ NO QSOJ; SB SV QPYFJQC NO SBV JVVJRAJ, EPZSRF P XSOOJYJRAJ UJBKJJR BWJ OYJJ PRX BWJ JRVQPHJX.

9. JSKTAFCG KMWFUMW BSC FB IMKRMICFSB SP PTRC, XZC FB CNM ZWM JTUM SP FCW IMKRMICFSB.

10. BSOIBLSFI CPTAAGAOVI CGSOP GAO

GFIV IFKKMAGAOV COY LO ISGA

YAPTAA IFKKMCOV HTAAYSG SH

CBVLSO XDLBD LI VDA PLHV SH

OCVFTA.

Answers on pages 108–109.

Ralph Waldo Emerson

(1803–1882)

1. CNX JBMAI XYLKCK UBM CNX XIRWHCLBP BU XHWN SHP.

2. ODYKXOE XB CY WCBY BCMZFN JTY YKF XOYFEZXYU DR UDTZ DIO GXON.

3. QATQTP BA UBGXTLHV; ALCLX QYQPSPL.

4. ZAW JXJWRDEKTQ RAN ECXJ SKPPJB, RAN ECXJ QCKTJB PASJDEKTQ JUPJ; CTB ZAW JXJWR DEKTQ RAN QCKT, RAN UAPJ PASJDEKTQ.

5. RIF YMFZVTMN TFRGY RIM RK RIF GZLAVZYY.

6. AOX UXTT F NFL AOSLYT DE YLDBT FGDQA OST PSEAQXT, AOX GXAAXE BX USYX OSN.

7. QHPPHV QH M CHPPBH KC PJH EKIH RG ZRYV GVKHCI PJMC JKE HDJR.

8. ZTU JIPQ LUGWLO JC MXLZVU XF MXLZVU; ZTU JIPQ GWQ ZJ TWMU W CLXUIO XF ZJ AU JIU.

9. UDY NG OBHIHOVDI HID VBD ONYLOEDYOD NG VBD LNOEDVP VN ABEOB VBDP JDRNYC.

10. LZFH VWVOK LZFVMMLJVZBV FUVOV LN D RHHO AULBU LN ZVWVO BMHNVR, FUOHXJU AULBU FUV BOVDFHO YDNNVN.

Answers on pages 109–110.

Benjamin Franklin

(1706–1790)

1. KISS FLEI CT PIGGIX GWBE KISS TBCF.

2. LOBNB TNB LONBB DTSLODAH DNSBFIX—TF GHI ESDB, TF GHI IGM, TFI NBTIU PGFBU.

3. WGHKBL IKARFBA GMBDNAKFH KL QKZG LKQPGU KH ARG YKHG.

4. DL RDGR UCNTX TVEL VY KLGIL GYX GR LGZL, WNZR YCR ZKLGJ GTT DL JYCUZ, YCP SNXQL GTT DL ZLLZ.

5. VUD UDESV PA VUD APPY MZ MC UMZ NPJVU, HJV VUD NPJVU PA VUD IMZD NEC MZ MC UMZ UDESV.

6. LENWN'M KCKN INBNFSNI HRL EN LEGL LWRMLM.

7. OVRB LIW MVRWG; OIB WGV UIILVB JV MNV, WGV HILFVB UGRHH JV DV NYYIBWRH.

8. IZQ DNTQ AWR PGWDT AEGQ WPLWRIWYQ MGEA ZNT QRQANQT, IZWR IZQ MEEX MGEA ZNT MGNQRPT.

9. KFKS TQU UDS ASPP-TWSO BCK MKFAN DFA UF IFKJSNN C JCQPU, FW CIMKFAPSOHS DZBNSPJ ZK CK SWWFW.

10. KCVT XL NSS LQ V QTNCXH, XLT WUCVI VXR LQ VX CXCBR.

Answers on pages 110–111.

Sigmund Freud

(1856–1939)

1. D UDL BRE ONHDUF VF NHUEQHO KNEU ARH BENXO EK BDSVLW ZELFZVECFLHFF.

2. 'VS' FJJYF VSQ QS JDMFQ FS ZKN KF CNJKYF KNJ HSVHJNVJC.

3. BXGCKM CXG BGXQTGB PXEK WVG DCMW QI GTGXL MGIMG.

4. WQ WG N RCVZUCLWNX BNHQ QYNQ JCUNSG SUXQ NONF WE QYU SVCEWET.

5. ZDQGNU GDQ OQWQD ESOEQDOQZ KBJM JDBWBGVBJBQU; KQ ZS OSJ GVVSK SFD UVQQH JS XQ ZBUJFDXQZ XL JDBIVQU.

6. VU VI NR JWMJFVJEZJ, CEH BEJ UB TLVZL V LCDJ QBGEH EB JWZJMUVBE, ULCU JDJFR HFJCN HJCXI TVUL ULJ HFJCNJF LVNIJXQ.

7. ZPN JZOZN KM JFNNV SXODOBZNNJ ZPN JNEXDGZL KM ZPN EGZOHNF ZPOZ AXJZ UN SXODHNH.

8. DIO MPDOKCKODBDMNP NH FKOBZE ME DIO KNQBG KNBF DN B APNJGOFTO NH DIO RPXNPEXMNRE BXDMWMDMOE NH DIO ZMPF.

9. CDGBJNUT NM B VNGOG EY NUYBUFNHG JGUFBH HNYG FABF ABM LGGU MWVGDMGCGC.

10. OKPHQG BMAP RHI EPDCKP WJP MQSKPGGMCFG CD H FPR OHI UYGW HG WJP EKMVVMHFZP CD WJP GWHKG IMPVOG WC WJP VMBJW CD WJP GYF.

Answers on page 111.

Georg Wilhelm Friedrich Hegel

(1770–1831)

Georg Wilhelm Friedrich Hegel

1. LVQ KQMRLV WYVVLA OQ YV QPQ YVG QYM FUAVQRR LJ QCQMPAZUVN.

2. KXHBI JZ LKGV AKEHSZ NH YBULBN K TJSLAM YBCYUYCJKA THYBN HQ UYLR.

3. DJT JTLTVDMMG ODQTU OTL OCVT ACMTVDLA; GCZAY KU DMEDGU RKUBCLATLATR.

4. KTX NMJMQZ XKTMBDN ARLNC MG GEMLMK MQ MKG KLWKT.

5. SJ WQCCQJ ASZX FUYFM CXVJD FMX VEUXXCXJF QZ VJ QTBXWF LSFM QYU WQJWXOFSQJ QZ SF.

6. XUNQNRNO XN TBNEF GA DUN GQN, DUN PEQM WTWECCM HGPN JQDG GWO PJQV ED DUN TEPN DJPN.

7. WLI SRKRVE ARI, QRTUSJ OIBPCQI PQ SRKRVE WLIJ OIPF RV WLITQISKIQ WLI EIFT ZD AIPWL.

8. DG AL AG TML LXF ONRLF, ORL MTPK LXF WDT LXDL LXATJG, MTPK XF—DTE MTPK OFBDRGF XF AG D LXATJATV OFATV—XDG CNFFEMW.

9. IJNNLUR HWD NQCFO UDGP EVNJN CDLCZCLMWGCOP CF JNHUKDCSNL WF VWZCDK COF BUFCOCZN WDL JNWG NQCFONDHN CD OVN LCZCDN ANCDK.

10. HXDVWR CV LYWASYL OWRFCLCWRCRS CLVXNP QCLY KXHPXOL PHXXFWI.

Answers on page 112.

Heraclitus

(c. 535–c. 475 B.C.)

1. JWMD ILCPONOA BYLT OYH HLCMD WOBLPTHCOBNOA.

2. YOOIOXY WP CWGR RBC VM SVUK OLXHK LJR PBJR GBHHGO.

3. PK PA TMBDPVMAA KC KCPW BK KSM ABLM KBAEA BVZ FM BWTBHA FMQPVVPVQ.

4. UZY'O DRZEZDNWE BO RBO PZNW.

5. KVPD FMVLI EFWX FY YJI VLI BJVR YJIZ KV LVY XLVB.

6. JL JR TXL ICLLCU NXU ZCXZYC LX DCL WYY LSWL LSCK EWTL.

7. VFU YXZ MZOF YGTSZV VHTC IF NZZS GULHGDFDT GUCZ VRUP CXGUNT GUSFFS.

8. ABZ VKGUH KL ABZ VCJFRY FX

KRZ CRH XBCGZH, MQA ABZ XUZZIFRY

AQGR CXFHZ ZCEB FRAK BFX IGFNCAZ

VKGUH.

9. KRKD CZO KCND CNK QGGN

BEVZKDDKD JGN YKZ EJ VPKEN DGXAD

OG ZGV XZOKNDVCZO VPK ACZMXCMK.

10. VW VP QFTU WG IVEQW FEFVLPW

XFPPVGL; IGT JQFWZHZT VW JFLWP

VW ACRP FW WQZ ZSXZLPZ GI WQZ

PGCD.

Answers on pages 112–113.

Horace (Quintus Horatius Flaccus)

(65–8 B.C.)

Horace

51

1. QX BZLL AKRL KC QWL PLMKYYKYM XB AKDQOL, UYE QX WUAL MXQ DKE XB BXZZI KC QWL PLMKYYKYM XB FKCEXN.

2. KJKCLHEAL QV AQVWEYPKYPKA OQPD DQV REP TYA KYJQKV DQV YKQIDHEC.

3. FAZWNFU, XA CAFU BX N BY NF YO XSFXSX, MAHCP N YBZDW MNZW ZWS KAO B JENSFP YBO TENFU.

4. ZRS PEPSF VJRQDKIG TCECIA DRQTD, VJPSP KSP KD BKIF VJRQDKIG VKDVPD.

5. OCOQR MTUJO DXH XGY SOOI SQASOU DOAJXY PQTPX SGUER.

6. JXZS VLG MUHG DUX WG QGNYGDV, UXF GCGX LG AUS MRYYGN YNJA U DJZF.

7. DLZCTDI TD BSVBJJ JCLWRY QB

LDB'J PWRB BEBD TD ZCB UWPJWTZ

LM ETPZWB.

8. 'CKD QKSBC CBGC NGVB DBZYXP

HNGDYQN BKHDNXU AE BKD ZJL QYXN

GLP DCGLPGQP.

9. D NDW'K LDQQUWVKK IVQVWIK WEG

EW LUK QXDTV EM DAEIV, ACG EW

LUK KGDGV EM NUWI.

10. HTAVB H JFCPNVAMCK, EAK RC VP

HQPA H NHNNQCK.

Answers on pages 113–114.

David Hume

(1711–1776)

1. YDFKGYR OI GZERGYI GB
ECBDXQFIXH GZNDBBGCXI.

2. RH JVRO, RH PHWO, RH RJGSD,
RH TOOP, RH LOO; VPP RJGL GL
SHRJGSX YAR RH COUKOGWO.

3. NW JYZJWOHW RTZU LMOZQI
NMOJM NW EY ZYL KWDOWHW.

4. DFNYBQ LY OSF ILYKBEFDX BZ
ODMOS BD ZNUYFSBBI.

5. YVISUB YVV BQJ ISCYV YU RJVV
YU PYBGCYV JOFVU SH QGIYP VFHJ
YCFUJ HCSI FEVJPJUU.

6. MG YRR XPH MGIMWHGXD QJ RMJH
BH QCVPX DXMRR XQ SFHDHFTH QCF
DEHSXMIMDA.

7. JFCM VCYB CMQCWV MLQ SMQL
QFC DLMVSXCWNQSLM, QFCWC SV ML
WLLZ BLW RWSXC LW FKZSYSQU.

8. LIH BGCBG LY EIZU DJADUB
YLJJLAB ZKG XLFFLC DCE CDZIHDJ
XLIHBG LY LIH SDBBNLCB.

9. IRKNZC PYBEUP SNCCERGC NGF
SKRFDBP RK SKPJPGU NBUERGC.

10. LZ KHD OZ KGISVEVZX OD GYI
GLM EHYCSP HMX EGCCVZP, OYS
MZNZI EZZC HMD HMWZI GI UHSIZX
ZTFZRS EIGK SUZ VMBYIVZP GE
GSUZIP.

Answers on pages 114–115.

William James

(1842–1910)

1. XJV VDXNMV CID, PJF GVVBU IBB DVVKU RT XHMDU, PNBB XIOV DFXJNDL IU ID VYHNSIBVDX GFM BNGV RHX XJV GHBDVUU FG BNSNDL NXUVBG.

2. SLV VCCFT L MIOC XPM JBT DBOO, LVF DBOO BVGCVY PVC BX PVC AC VPY EBGCV.

3. EJM ECBEJN DHTTRE LMDRGM ECBM EPAA RBC SHPEJ JHN GHOM EJMG NR.

4. UXUQF EUZ JMML XUQJDHBVUN NMKU EUZ TMETUOI, ZRBTR JUTMKUN BKOMQIDEI BE OQMOMQIBME IM IRU PNU IRDI TDE JU KDWU MS BI.

5. BYHN YK DZN BDZX NTEYZX DH EWN HGPYE DH EWN EGNN DH CZDVBNSXN.

6. B UGEEQI VEAKWTIGEA WKRWKI JBIDQVI IDK GAZBTTBQE QN WKGP, RKEVBEK HQTTBLBPBIBKT BE IDK JQWPA.

7. SC SA AOPMPSASQR IDJ ADDQ U FHASPH JSXX FSH DL SQUQSCSDQ SL SC YH QHGHP LHF.

8. BXNGN YV IQ DQVVYEZN DQYIB QW CYNH WGQK HXYPX BXN HQGZU PJI JDDNJG JI JEVQZSBNZA VYIMZN WJPB.

9. LUKY ZBPQH KY TBBH, ZN FJYL YOR, YKVAN KL KY ZUOL ZN FOCN KL, OVH ZN YUOQQ FOCN KL TBBH.

10. FXIFQWVZ IXV XITM HYAGQ YZ XOQL VBQ CPW XJ TAJQ, NYV SQ LQOPTYQ TAJQ NM VBQAL YZQ.

Answers on pages 115–116.

Immanuel Kant
(1724–1804)

1. VSZLZ DCH RZ HE GEJRV VSCV
CNN EJL THEYNZGKZ RZKQHP YQVS
ZFXZLQZHDZ.

2. HDMNIDHY KOHDMNH FMRHJRH WZJ
JBUHP, ORHNOHOMRY KOHDMNH
FMRFJUHY WZJ SGORL.

3. OM AWD KBZHD HWLZJQ WBUD
KDBHDQ AL DGOHA B SLSDIA CDMLED,
AWD DMMDKA XLZJQ IDUDE WBUD
KLSD AL CD.

4. WEE QOJ XOZWP TPUTCXA GWTEU
WU UQQP WU KF JFWVX DWUTV
BQKFJU QJ GWVOEATFU.

5. PYFBWLYV LYFEPA BH
JBHFBLIEBHGAJ QPWO FGA PAHF WQ
LYFEPA KZ HAFFBLI BFHAVQ YL ALJ.

6. MII JPY MHHAUSXHP BAPPCVJ VB
LUII HV HNPJKPIWPK.

7. MBDG XNFABYG IN FEG PNFA NKU
FUZGAEIBUZVUY.

8. SASX NE QSLQKS ISCS XLV
BLRQSKKSG DW NXVSCXOK GNUUSXV
VL UMDRNV VL VZS BLSCBNLX LE
QMDKNB KOIU, IOC ILMKG QCLGMBS
VZS UORS SEESBV ECLR LMVUNGS.

9. UZ T JXIORS VTSSRW JIRQX WYTW
T WYUSA XGUOWO, YX FTP TWWXFJW
WR JIRQX WYTW UW BRXO SRW
XGUOW.

10. X EQKAWBRUAC TXF OQWW MBR
XC QCG RA XBRAYEXRUY GQLMARULT
XCG RA EXMXYUABL AE
LQWD-LQQJUCN AMMEQLLUAC, ZBR UR
OUWW CQKQE MEAGBYQ X REBQ
EQDAET UC OXFL AD RIUCJUCN.

Answers on page 116.

Soren Kierkegaard

(1813–1855)

1. TFM ARIG UFTC TFMIMBQ PMQTYM
UFTCZFL HFJGNZFL MBIM.

2. LZJ PLJE ZLQ GJNTZ MJBEQTZN BQ
PBDZ GWQ BQ EWZEJQ.

3. CDFRPM, ORLD B NEPFIDTMNSTZ,
XSZDM PG BCBRFMN NED ARFI.

4. RH YAWVRYAU SLYXZ KLVYXQA HL
QYRAGA; RH YAWVRYAU YAZRQRLVU
KLVYXQA HL YAILRKA.

5. JNEQVNS BH OUQ ENNO NZ RKK
QIBK, RYV BO BH OUBH PUBTU SLHO
JQ FQXO RO R VBHORYTQ.

6. WXR HNMR UNB QJHJW UNBMYRQI,
WXR HNMR IRMWJQR UNB ZRENHR JP
JPARPWJNP.

7. WVO OPO YTWV YVTFV PIJ DIIU QW AOQDTWP LJKW FISKWQSWDP MO FVQSROZ.

8. LMNUJ QUCHN UBN XPS XGVWV BGV WPSN DQ BGV NMC JPCCDB KVCVBWPBV.

9. X SXO IBT WXOOTA LRMJWR SRO WXOOTA LXKR ABRS RVABRY.

10. XNHSEPWR CPW CSMCTZ MWSS-GWNCIWE CZ SYRJ CZ FNWT CPW WRAYTHRJ FNWLZWSIWZ.

Answers on page 117.

Lao Tzu

(c. 570–490 B.C.)

1. EBWC JRXB NOB SXAEMBZPXL DXOIVC OL LIAR KEXL IMWZBXLL DXAENX SXOWZVC.

2. MGD RYEBK PEYDE DR HYEB OEB GWONJ MYTT NWOIG YHHDNJOTYJZ.

3. KDUAZVZ XHVFK EVZ UHW TDUZ; TDUZ XHVFK EVZ UHW KDUAZVZ.

4. QCTIT ZJ HR EFVFYZQX KITFQTI QCFH VZKCQVX THKFKZHK ZH NFI.

5. PUOT LUO KOCKZO AC TCL ROQM PUQL LUOG CBNUL LC ROQM, LUQL PUEHU EY LUOEM NMOQL AMOQA PEZZ DO CT LUOX.

6. XDH LMBNJVB DSB KMBBSHYB MYF NRVYB NDJL NH FJJFB HP WSYFYJBB, SB AVJMNJV NDMY M WSYA.

7. OK GOQ CYAONCD VHQTYRKR YR RIHK NQ BKKV FIN CYNNCK EJYNO.

8. MG AMW HQWAI WUMGS RGQ LI NLIZGSQLQT; MG AMW HQWAI MLRIGPO LI LQUGPPLTGQU.

9. XJ JXQ DIX TLX AHKE ZOTQIB MQUZ.

10. AO KAC NMJQGOG AQPGOXZ POMQEG XQEEXO JNNMOBQJEQCS.

Answers on pages 117–118.

John Locke

(1632–1704)

1. UPSJOV SJ QNSJU GBVU VUWJI WJI AWRR YF UPDSN HTJ THNUP, HN UPD NDWIDN'V AWJEF.

2. WZD KJQHXD WZJW EG GDW CV EQ CG GZEQDG SIENZW DQBCNZ OBI JXX BCI VCIVBGDG.

3. IOTYHW QRZ UTQODW QTW DX HROYWZ YBQY YBWJ QTW GQMMWZ XEYWR SJ YBW DQPW RQPW.

4. HYY ZVHZ SC NCKRLC RK AUYF ZA IC VHXXF.

5. MQHDWDU UDVRDXFK HZ MQJF CJKKDK NZ QNK HMZ ANZB XJZZHF ANKK NF.

6. MSR WKBMNPRC OPULI KI YNP VKIOC UPR TUKO KI JUOKIQ BYTYPC, UIO KJ IYM CYVRMKVRC PRJPRCSRO GUIKCS UIO OKCUWWRUP.

7. N ZREYT MR GKTYDM MWY RZYTNMKUY BNDSIMKYH MR ORMKRP RT TYHM KP ZNTMKDSINT KPHMNPDYH KH MWNM EWKDW EY DNII MWY EKII.

8. XFU'C TIEUWETSFC, UGBEGUC OUN IFSECQFC OIF CG NEHHFIFUB, BQOB EB EC QOIN BG HEUN O DGGZ PQEWQ TSFOCFC GI NECTSFOCFC OSS XFU.

9. DWDHN VSDY STD GOJX SUMDV OJ OSV YHQLHDVV SQFUHX MJQFEDXLD GUMDV VQGD XOVPQWDHN, FTOPT OV JQS QJEN JDF, ICS STD IDVS SQQ, RQH STD SOGD US EDUVS.

10. RW RJ IG ULNBW KJN WI WAN JBRZIL WI VHIS WAN ZNHUWA IG ARJ ZRHN, WAIKUA AN TBHHIW SRWA RW GBWAIY BZZ WAN CNDWAJ IG WAN ITNBH.

Answers on pages 118–119.

Friedrich Wilhelm Nietzsche

(1844–1900)

1. VYX SXQJEYXQ TPQE PL SIQ
HQQIPKQE VU VYX GLVATQNMQ.

2. IRT UKIRCKUM MKIRDF CTIL IRU IG
IRT ZXDROM LYUK UKO MXVO
QOHOMMYUJ XM UKO GTRYU IRU IG
UKO UTOO.

3. JNV TXUEEUB HKU VU CWNVUKE,
DKNIQBUB VU CWNV JNV SN CUUD
EQXUWS XNWZ UWNPZJ!

4. QU QB G WTTX UVQLW UVGU SZ
XT LTUVQLW NTY SVQDV SZ GYZ LTU
BUYTLW ZLTCWV.

5. WAJ KGGOJO WAJ NJNGOT GU
NRSEXSZ ARV MJJS, WAJ NGOJ
WJOOXMCJ ARLJ MJJS XWV BDVWGNV.

6. VLNSN UB PX DNCBV RUVLXFV
ZSFNEVH, CB TCP'B NPVUSN LUBVXSH
CVVNBVB.

7. VHH PDUWPDFWU WZVW VMG DAW
VHHAXGK BMGG YHVS WQMD PDXVMK.

8. XWPBP ATQ NP QL RLYNX XWTX
NTR ALQOAKPQAP KO T OKAGQPOO,
NYX OL, KQ T OPQOP, KO IBPFQTQAS.

9. OUU SNNL RGJISE GOZK OR NIK
RJPK FKKI WNIEJLKCKL KZJU; KZKCA
NCJSJIOU EJI GOE, OR ENPK XNJIR,
RYCIKL JIRN OI NCJSJIOU ZJCRYK.

10. DOO IWNDC CPXHIV ZNWXVP BT
CPNXW BYH DQQBWJ, MS DH DQC BT
VNOT-QDHQNOODCXBH: VB CPN ODY
BT OXTN JNQWNNV.

Answers on pages 119–120.

Blaise Pascal

(1623–1662)

1. NUI HULYI AKJKDYI HLXYF KJ DCN QV KESIXBISNKDYI JSIBG KV NUI QESYI DLJLE LO VQNCXI.

2. RGTGAQXY RGYXKUGW BVG UGSFKPG YK SKTC BY XJGO YGGP FBIBRSG KA VGIBOPGTX; BAXGV XJBX CVBXQXEWG XEVTY XK VGYGTXPGTX.

3. NAOU CJB TCGU MCJ MTCJYU GTU HCMU AH LDWGEMU.

4. HJ JHG MBGUNM JD VM WH JVC BCGMGHPG UM WH JVC UAMGHPG.

5. MAT YITS NZJI QIUIBQC MB GBMXZBF XPIKPIT KPI CMAN ZC HMTKRN MT ZHHMTKRN.

6. SRU'F ABORJUOFF NMOF MU QMF LZXOB ZD JQZHAQJ.

7. E TEH'K ZVDUM GK UV RB TBEKYDBJ HVU RC MGK KFEKTVJGO BNNVDUK RYU RC MGK BSBDCJEC PGNB.

8. KPYVX XVWPMA HT XGW VRUVFT VBIVXQHXC; HW QGYAT VXB CGAT.

9. ANBYNNP WU MPX TNII QL TNMJNP BTNLN OU QPIG IODN, MPX BTMB OU BTN ZQUB DLMROIN BTOPR OP BTN YQLIX.

10. JNL LJLBEZJH KP JNZEWO ZE ZJOLCP KB ZE WKI DTOJ QKEPKTEI KTB YBZLP ITBUJZKE.

Answers on pages 120–121.

Plato

(c. 427–347 B.C.)

1. FI FL XYYK IY CEJU IWMU
QUDFUGL, QMI QEK IY QU FB UWWYW.

2. EV EO GKVVEPTX IKJ VKSXKWX
DMK YWKDV VKSXOMEWC WKO OK
YWKD DMZO MX YWKDV?

3. COXP BK GN FN JPC RCONGLC BK
JPC JPFDMN JPOJ OLC ODV OLC DBJ.

4. TDC FJD TDNU ECNSCZC AVJG TDC
SB CQYCWSCDFSDH JDR GVSB SB
JNAJUB GWPC.

5. TJIJCT BVPFOLQB LDQ
VZZVFLSCJLW KVF GJBPSBBJVC JB
XJHQ TJIJCT POIOXFW LDQ
VZZVFLSCJLW LV KJTDL VC XQIQX
TFVSCG.

6. JN VACL BKJ UA LAKJOJRISE POVGNSV DJNPEAHRA NI PGKV OV ZVKJHZ INC.

7. BOU CX AKJ BJOXIWJ SQ OEE AKCUDX—SQ AKJ AKCUDX AKOA OWJ, AKOA AKJV OWJ; SQ AKJ AKCUDX AKOA OWJ USA, AKOA AKJV OWJ USA.

8. ADAFGIJCSO UJCKJ UA EAMKFCQA YM 'QACSO' CM YKIBYHHG CS IJA TFWKAMM WL QACSO OASAFYIAE YM Y FAMBHI WL VWDAVASI YSE KJYSOA YSE VBIBYH VCZIBFA.

9. VBN GPZJNYY ZI HNTNPEVMZT—VBEV MY, EGGEPNTV CNMTH—MY E PNYOSV ZI JBETHN: COV FNYVPOJVMZT—VBEV MY, TZV CNMTH—MY E PNYOSV ZI MTEJVMQMVX.

10. LOBAB IAB LFG QVEZR GD HOIEPB,

FOVHO KIM UB ZVRLVEPXVROBZ EGL

UM LOBVA DABTXBEHM GD

GHHXAABEHB UXL UM LOBVA CGFBAR:

GEB VR IHLVWB, LOB GLOBA

CIRRVWB.

Answers on pages 121–122.

Will Rogers

(1879–1935)

1. LMNJTX YUQ CUP TUOX TJIX WLUIP JKY JD YCX UTXILNUM HXJHWX YCUM ZJWD CUP.

2. X LCEJYJGJXB JT BCY XT BXSSCR-PJBMOM XT KO WCSGOT KJPTOEW YC AO.

3. GF KQRXVNITV HYHQ'N RIGX IQ NUX GKFCOISXT PLN NUXF GXN NUX PIKN.

4. N'P BGVOXB CX BNJOV VOGR BXYSCANHGR.

5. VK IAXD FVSZ VN BADFP JGIFPVGU, FDJOZM QI JVD. VK GAF, IAX SVUPF YXNF JN BZMM BJMT.

6. ZDEBNEBN I VYQH EZ IOO VENJR DJHB PYLV BHTF IEB'R EB ER.

7. VTIITZWEN UTEYG TE YQBG PYIUB WB Q TEY-ZQG PWADYP PT PKY HTTIKTFBY.

8. LQDN I XIQ PLTHV I SEMTRD LYYRDN PN RV IMVLTEFNTZ QL WLLH YLC PLQNVF KLCB.

9. ZIO MVNS Z NZI EZI'M EANS ZIF QSMMBS PVMW OAL PVMWALM JDVIYVIY WVQ BZPOSD, PWO, BAAU ALM GAD WVN.

10. FXNVUEF OFY GNINV RBYK F DFV, BV DBG F EBGPNVNGEN.

Answers on page 122.

Bertrand Russell

(1872–1970)

1. YTDLMTV OH O POSZTD AI URVOI
YLUOKATD UOH DLSLAKLM, AI VQ
TWAIATI, POD GLHH OZZLIZATI ZUOI
AZ MLHLDKLH.

2. FSFDM ULR PNYQV QKAF IN XF
CNV, KJ KI PFDF BNGGKXQF; GNUF
JFP JKRV KI VKJJKHYQI IN LVUKI IZF
KUBNGGKXKQKIM.

3. OCZATJCU CYYOQEQJGATJ TN
ICJDQOG AG JQVQGGCOX; NQCO AG
JTZ.

4. UTQLUTML, OUTF BTF QYUAUL BAV
BPP VQQVTLUBP LH B KSPP PUKV;
VBMI IBQ ULQ HJT VGMVPPVTMV BTF
ULQ HJT MHAASYLUHT.

5. XV XGNMVX BGJ AYAC JV YMCNQVQJ GJ AGTI RAWMAYAJ MNJAWE, GXH XVXA BGJ AYAC JV BMTLAH GJ AGTI RAWMAYAJ NIA VNIAC.

6. YJ HRZI YQI MJPAB PITEOPIH UROYQ RLB NJEPRVI; UROYQ OL PIRHJL, RLB NJEPRVI YJ DPJNAROS MQRY PIRHJL HQJMH YJ KI YPEI.

7. WFQGCMQGW, MH LMFXW QGU JOG CF PG PGZMGTGY, KFY'W QGOEMGW JOG EXOMFXWZS WGZGECMTG.

8. ATCTA KGH URDQSGKP LSDKPTBI KDR RYWKPPI GRARQQKDI BS K ZSSH XSDPH.

9. SOQQL DA FDUUQUURDG ZRHH SODZ HQUU ZPQG CPQOQ RU GD AQYO DA LQUCRCMCRDG.

10. UFEIDBDUFQMB FOGQ DJIN

EJZQMUMQZQP ZFQ VDMIP EJ

GOMEDSB VONB, YSZ ZFQ MQOI ZOBL

EB ZD OIZQM EZ.

Answers on pages 122–123.

Jean-Paul Sartre

(1905–1980)

1. YNPG MVTGVQUFVTNXT UHM IDHA
APQ VT QHG UDXPGXD IDXXMHA WFG
UDXPGXD LHYXD.

2. DCQ RQNE JNQQOMI DM SWWQGD
MN NQPQWD DCQ JSVKQ LK LDKQVJ
WNQSDLRQ.

3. UBVTQAVTU QLT BSKTNQ BO
FXFCTWTUU XAJJ ST UBVTQLAWI AW
QLT XBCJM, UBVTQAVTU AQ XAJJ ST
QLT UTJO.

4. JOHDFHQ FL DWJ
DNBQLSHNOBDFHQ HS DWJ XHNTP.

5. ZUGQ B DPGNPWPNNWK GBI
QAZGYFN BN IKNPWV, QUGQ ZUBDU B
GI EAQ, IK AZE JANNBCBWBQBPN.

6. OSMQYIAHI NELN MNEIB WIMWYI IUTJN, LSA LBI FMSJFTMZJ, TJ WLBN LSA WLBFIY MV MZB MQS LQLBISIJJ MV MZBJIYGIJ.

7. GH GW HUY FYEHU XS MUGRXWXMUO GS GH PXVSJWYW HUY HTJY DGHU HUY PXVBGVPGVA.

8. F ZMYY FRX BDRIBJDEI PYJRH BFRRDV PY TDIIYIIYX.

9. KXVFUKO UZ ZSCNIYPSXSZ UY UV UZ CRIV XY R IRVUXKRP CPRK.

10. XHWDK DLPRJKT WHTP IO BRCRBOB RKPJ DK RKTRBO DKB DK JHPTRBO—SXDP D WDK RKPOKBT, DKB SXDP XO BJOT.

Answers on pages 123–124.

Arthur Schopenhauer

(1788–1860)

1. SK FEUK COKEPQ; PED JMI MLO SFMNK NGXK YK E COKEP?

2. EBOD CQK KUDCST CUD EDCGDT ZO NFD TCSD AZZH.

3. HMNFCHS CD NM ZA FOL KMW SMGL ZQN UALCMPWCNB.

4. PLOXC DQ DLC QGBOYRGS ZRY LOM WRNAXDS QW FYQPXCBUC OM R XRZI DQ XOULDCY LOM IRDL, DQ R ZRY QW UCYOAM OD OM DLC MAY PLONL GCKCRXM DLC PQGXB.

5. EOTT OV UXG UXOPF-OP-OUVGTN, UXG OPPGI LKPUGPU, UXG GVVGPLG KN UXG EKITS.

6. RUHL, WKL EUOUNRL PIZRJ, WKL XKLSIVLSIS, UO ISRA WKL VUZZIZ IH WKL PURR.

7. LQGI QA SQHI DY BYZIDAQYK
ALNIDG, DYW LMI JNIAIYL D NRZH RY
UMQZM LMI ALNIDG PNIDHA QLAIST,
PBL WRIA YRL ZDNNX DUDX UQLM QL.

8. VCPJA VDMUD XPOKPJK DLX
MJNIMURKQ YZPJ OK EB JP OKLJX
KJRMRIKX OK RP MJNIMUR VCPJA
YZPJ DMO.

9. UAGAJJLKF LJ KNA VLUTSMR MP
UBKEZA; PZAASMR LJ KNA VLUTSMR
MP TZBGA.

10. QHKB KBW WTIWAKHPS PZ VNS, SP
EWHSX QPSRWCF NK HKF PQS
WTHFKWSIW; EGK HK HF KP KBWV NJJ
FP VGIB N VNKKWC PZ IPGCFW KBNK
KBWO RP SPK PEFWCUW HK.

Answers on pages 124–125.

Baruch Spinoza

(1632–1677)

1. FLFYGHQJAW NQJKQ JX, JX FJHQFY JA JHXFDV BY JA UABHQFY.

2. NDC MHVXTCSQC VP GH CPPCYN SCWCHSR LWVH GHS BHKVTKCR NDC MHVXTCSQC VP NDC YGLRC.

3. ATG NRYY XEHHMA CG XEYYGI E OPGG XEZFG, CZA XEH MHYB CG XEYYGI HGXGFFEPB.

4. LO RLU XJIPXKOY SLIS LO IBBOWSY USLOVY RXSL ZUE UV YUVVUR RXCC KOWOYYIVXCE TO IBBOWSOQ RXSL ZUE UV YUVVUR.

5. PF JOJSH CBULF UPFY KGUJ PYJLK LSJ LYJXBLMJ, LFY GMCJSK UBMPWLMJY LFY NGFIBKJY.

6. CGS ABDD UVR CGS BVCSDDSEC UJS IVS UVR CGS YUOS.

7. VRJYKH CT CZGYKRTKH JVYQAEV
YKJAYZ QI VRJYKH, XAJ URD XK
HKTJYQDKH XD BQWK.

8. NQ XOUACUQ ZFCDF CL N ENLLCUQ
DXNLXL AU RX N ENLLCUQ NL LUUQ
NL ZX KUHO N DJXNH NQY YCLACQDA
CYXN UK CA.

9. CRU RBJWY JZYF IWYYGC PU
WPTGNBCUNX FUTCMGXUF EZCR CRU
PGFX, PBC TGJUCRZYH GV ZC
MUJWZYT ERZIR ZT UCUMYWN.

10. FYI GVZIA VJ RVN HX YHX IXXIPQI
HFXIKJ.

Answers on pages 125–126.

Henry David Thoreau

(1817–1862)

Henry David Thoreau

1. DN DU LSN HQQ CSSAU NYHN HKM HU OFQQ HU NYM KMHOMKU.

2. CUF WYQGFBMF QM XQOFB CURY JWB GQFX JH QC.

3. NTPATR VW HRYTD MHD GTTQ PW UTOO PW MATD MHD NTPYW.

4. YTPHP CO QF FNFH OF ELN LO YTLY VTCDT LHCOPO IHFX RFFNQPOO YLCQYPN.

5. OE OZ EYQ WACAXOTAZ NSP EYQ POZZOINEQP MYT ZQE EYQ BNZYOTSZ MYOFY EYQ YQXP ZT POWOJQSEWG BTWWTM.

6. BW QTJLBTJL WLP'C CPZX WL BSJC PTYBS JC LWB T STYRCSJA GKB T ATCBJQP JX HP ZJOP CJQAZI TLR HJCPZI.

7. MT YSXI ADZXD AI XSM HZJI KT S
GSKKIF AZNN PKISE LP PT AINN SK
NSPK SP KDI KFLKD.

8. MFXE ZUWHUNX XV MFX, F
OUKZGUQ XEKX XEUZU MKW GVX JTNE
QFLLUZUGNU AUXMUUG XEU EKOL KGQ
XEU MEVOU.

9. WG ZWH JFUBFYCTFUWGU BWG
BLTG UKAHL HX WFU XHHJ MKY
YGAGL IG K CVTBBHY; WG ZWH JHGU
YHB MKYYHB IG HBWGLZFUG.

10. DY LOLXW YLDYST YLLZY PLYU US
JY MT MUY UJXT, YS UFL BSZMTC MT
SA YQXMTC MY RMGL UFL BXLDUMST
SA BSYZSY SJU SA BFDSY DTI UFL
XLDRMKDUMST SA UFL CSRILT DCL.

Answers on page 126.

100

Answers

Aesop

1. 'Tis good advice to look before we leap.

2. 'Tis the part of a wise man to prefer things necessary before matters of curiosity, ornament or pleasure.

3. Charity begins at home, they say; and most people are kind to their neighbors for their own sakes.

4. Without good nature and gratitude, men had as good live in a wilderness as in a society.

5. Action is the business of life, and there's no thought of ever coming to the end of our journey in time if we sleep by the way.

6. There are no snares so dangerous as those that are laid for us under the name of good offices.

7. One foolish word is enough to spoil a good cause, and 'tis many a man's fortune to cut his own throat with his own arguments.

8. It is according to prudence, as well as nature, to pay that honor to your parents, that you expect your children should pay to you.

9. Let no man despair in adversity, nor presume in prosperity, for all things are changeable.

10. Watch for the opportunities of doing things, for there's nothing well done but what's done in season.

Aristotle

1. Small bits of good fortune or of its opposite clearly do

not effect the balance of life on one side or the other.

2. Not everything that is visible depends upon light for its visibility.

3. If the soul is moved, the most probable view is that what moves it is sensible things.

4. Happiness is good activity, not amusement.

5. The science of the good for man is politics.

6. Loving is more of the essence of friendship than being loved.

7. It may be said that every individual man, and all men in common, aim at a certain end which determines what they choose and what they avoid.

8. Honor is the token of a man's being famous for doing good.

9. Beauty varies with the time of life.

10. The end and the means towards it may come about by chance.

St. Augustine

1. As a candle is a light in the night, so the just man is a light in the darkness of this world.

2. Wisdom teaches, the soul repents, the flesh sheds tears.

3. To burn is the punishment of the wicked, to give light is the happiness of the just.

4. The peace of all things is the tranquillity of order.

5. It is not the body, but the corruptibility of the body, that is burdensome to the soul.

6. Let us build together our cities on faith and love, and they will be invincible.

7. Every man seeks peace by waging war, but no man seeks war by making peace.

8. Neither by the fabulous nor by the civil theology does any one obtain eternal life.

9. As long as you burden your heart with things of earth, are you not courting heaviness of heart?

10. They, who are destined to die, need not be careful to inquire what death they are to die, but into what place death will usher them.

Francis Bacon

1. A man that is young in years, may be old in hours, if he has lost no time.

2. Wives are young men's mistresses, companions for middle age, and old men's nurses.

3. The greatest trust, between man and man, is the trust of giving counsel.

4. There is surely no greater wisdom, than well to time the beginning, and onset of things.

5. Riches are for spending; and spending for honor and good actions.

6. I cannot call riches better than the baggage of virtue.

7. Praise is the reflection of virtue.

8. The winning of honor is but the revealing of a man's virtue and worth, without disadvantage.

9. Whatever has been proved by authorities is determined even more certainly from the experience of any man.

10. The way of salvation is one, although there may be many steps; but wisdom is the way to salvation.

Martin Buber

1. Work is made for man, not man for work.

2. The tree of life can never be disjointed from the tree of knowledge for both have one and the same root.

3. Each religion is a house of the human soul longing for God.

4. A thinker who begins anew without daring to begin anew in all earnest must fail.

5. As long as man perceives the self as an object, he is not united.

6. Faith is the victorious and triumphant message.

7. The great peace is something essentially different from the absence of war.

8. Write only what you want to communicate; write so that it is communicated.

9. Our being itself is an inheritance from our forebears that we bequeath to our children.

10. The world of man without the soul of it in addition is no human world; but also the soul of man without the world in addition is no human soul.

Buddha

1. Little by little must the minds of men be trained for higher truths.

2. As all earthen vessels made by the potter end in being broken, so is the life of mortals.

3. Those who fail to aspire for the truth have missed the purpose of life.

4. Truth is the essence of life, for truth endureth beyond the death of the body.

5. A kind man who makes good use of his wealth is rightly said to possess a great treasure; but the miser who hoards up his riches will have no profit.

6. Purify your hearts and cease to kill; that is true religion.

7. Perfect peace can dwell only where all vanity has disappeared.

8. Our good or evil deeds follow us continually like shadows.

9. Surely if living creatures saw the results of all their deeds, they would turn away from them in disgust.

10. There is no evil but what flows from self.

Samuel Clemens

1. Water taken in moderation cannot hurt anybody.

2. A man never reaches that dizzy height of wisdom when he can no longer be led by the nose.

3. France has neither winter nor summer nor morals— apart from these drawbacks it is a fine country.

4. Wit is the sudden marriage of ideas which before their union were not perceived to have any relation.

5. My books are water; those of the great geniuses are wine. Everybody drinks water.

6. Irreverence is the champion of liberty and its only sure defense.

7. Love seems the swiftest, but it is the slowest of all growths.

8. If man could be crossed with the cat it would improve man, but it would deteriorate the cat.

9. An occasional compliment is necessary to keep up one's self-respect.

10. Be careless in your dress if you must, but keep a tidy soul.

Confucius

1. Respect the heavenly and earthly spirits and keep them at a distance.

2. A man who has committed a mistake and doesn't correct it, is committing another mistake.

3. A gentleman does not praise a man on the basis of what he says, nor does he deny the truth of what one says because he dislikes the person who says it.

4. Do not worry about people not knowing your ability, but worry that you have not got it.

5. A gentleman blames himself, while a common man blames others.

6. If a man would be severe toward himself and generous toward others, he would never arouse resentment.

7. A man who does not think and plan long ahead will find trouble right by his door.

8. Repay kindness with kindness, but repay evil with justice.

9. It is man that makes truth great, and not truth that makes man great.

10. Only the highest and lowest characters don't change.

John Dewey

1. The more striving the more attainments, perhaps; but also assuredly the more needs and the more disappointments.

2. The more we do and the more we accomplish, the more the end is vanity and vexation.

3. Humility is more demanded at our moments of triumph than at those of failure.

4. Perception of things as they are is but a stage in the process of making them different.

5. Intelligence becomes ours in the degree in which we use it and accept responsibility for consequences.

6. A free man would rather take his chance in an open world than be guaranteed in the closed world.

7. Choice is an element in freedom and there can be no choice without unrealized and precarious possibilities.

8. Variety is more than the spice of life; it is largely of its essence, making a difference between the free and the enslaved.

9. Morality resides not in perception of fact, but in the use made of its perception.

10. Conscious agreements among men must supplement and in some degree supplant freedom of action which is the gift of nature.

Ralph Waldo Emerson

1. The world exists for the education of each man.

2. Nothing is at last sacred but the integrity of your own mind.

3. Insist on yourself; never imitate.

4. For everything you have missed, you have gained something else; and for every thing you gain, you lose something.

5. Our strength grows out of our weakness.

6. The less a man thinks or knows about his virtues, the better we like him.

7. Better be a nettle in the side of your friend than his echo.

8. The only reward of virtue is virtue; the only way to have a friend is to be one.

9. Men of character are the conscience of the society to which they belong.

10. Into every intelligence there is a door which is never closed, through which the Creator passes.

Benjamin Franklin

1. Well done is better than well said.

2. There are three faithful friends—an old wife, an old dog, and ready money.

3. Genius without education is like silver in the mine.

4. He that would live in peace and at ease, must not speak all he knows, nor judge all he sees.

5. The heart of the fool is in his mouth, but the mouth of the wise man is in his heart.

6. There's none deceived but he that trusts.

7. Fear not death; for the sooner we die, the longer shall we be immortal.

8. The wise man draws more advantage from his enemies, than the fool from his friends.

9. None but the well-bred man knows how to confess a fault, or acknowledge himself in an error.

10. Hear no ill of a friend, nor speak any of an enemy.

Sigmund Freud

1. A man who dreams is removed from the world of waking consciousness.

2. 'No' seems not to exist so far as dreams are concerned.

3. Dreams are derived from the past in every sense.

4. It is a proverbial fact that dreams melt away in the morning.

5. Dreams are never concerned with trivialities; we do not allow our sleep to be disturbed by trifles.

6. It is my experience, and one to which I have found no exception, that every dream deals with the dreamer himself.

7. The state of sleep guarantees the security of the citadel that must be guarded.

8. The interpretation of dreams is the royal road to a knowledge of the unconscious activities of the mind.

9. Dreaming is a piece of infantile mental life that has been superseded.

10. Dreams give way before the impressions of a new day just as the brilliance of the stars yields to the light of the sun.

Georg Wilhelm Friedrich Hegel

1. One person cannot be an eye and ear witness of everything.

2. Among us each labors to invent a purely individual point of view.

3. Age generally makes men more tolerant; youth is always discontented.

4. The living ethical world is spirit in its truth.

5. In common life truth means the agreement of an object with our conception of it.

6. Whenever we speak of the one, the many usually come into our mind at the same time.

7. The living die, simply because as living they bear in themselves the germ of death.

8. As it is not the brute, but only the man that thinks, only he—and only because he is a thinking being—has freedom.

9. Freedom can exist only where individuality is recognized as having its positive and real existence in the divine being.

10. Reason is thought conditioning itself with perfect freedom.

Heraclitus

1. Much learning does not teach understanding.

2. Seekers of gold dig up much earth and find little.

3. It is weariness to toil at the same tasks and be always beginning.

4. Man's character is his fate.

5. Dogs alone bark at the one whom they do not know.

6. It is not better for people to get all that they want.

7. Men who love wisdom must be good inquirers into many things indeed.

8. The world of the waking is one and shared, but the sleeping turn aside each into his private world.

9. Eyes and ears are poor witnesses for men if their souls do not understand the language.

10. It is hard to fight against passion; for whatever it wants it buys at the expense of the soul.

Horace

1. To flee vice is the beginning of virtue, and to have got rid of folly is the beginning of wisdom.

2. Everybody is discontented with his lot and envies his neighbor.

3. Nothing, so long as I am in my senses, would I match with the joy a friend may bring.

4. For every thousand living souls, there are as many thousand tastes.

5. Every judge who has been bribed weighs truth badly.

6. Only the sage can be perfect, and even he may suffer from a cold.

7. Nothing in excess should be one's rule even in the pursuit of virtue.

8. 'Tis right that each should measure himself by his own rule and standard.

9. A man's happiness depends not on his place of abode, but on his state of mind.

10. Avoid a questioner, for he is also a tattler.

David Hume

1. Nothing we imagine is absolutely impossible.

2. To hate, to love, to think, to feel, to see; all this is nothing but to perceive.

3. We conceive many things which we do not believe.

4. Reason is the discovery of truth or falsehood.

5. Almost all the moral as well as natural evils of human life arise from idleness.

6. In all the incidents of life we ought still to preserve our skepticism.

7. When self enters not into the consideration, there is no room for pride or humility.

8. Our sense of duty always follows the common and natural course of our passions.

9. Morals excite passions and produce or prevent actions.

10. We may be mortified by our own faults and follies, but never feel any anger or hatred except from the injuries of others.

William James

1. The entire man, who feels all needs by turns, will take nothing as an equivalent for life but the fulness of living itself.

2. Man needs a rule for his will, and will invent one if one be not given.

3. The truths cannot become true till our faith has made them so.

4. Every new book verbalizes some new concept, which becomes important in proportion to the use that can be made of it.

5. Life is one long eating of the fruit of the tree of knowledge.

6. I cannot understand regret without the admission of real, genuine possibilities in the world.

7. It is surprising how soon a desire will die of inanition if it be never fed.

8. There is no possible point of view from which the world can appear an absolutely single fact.

9. This world is good, we must say, since it is what we make it, and we shall make it good.

10. Concepts not only guide us over the map of life, but we revalue life by their use.

Immanuel Kant

1. There can be no doubt that all our knowledge begins with experience.

2. Thoughts without content are empty, intuitions without concepts are blind.

3. If the cause should have ceased to exist a moment before, the effect would never have come to be.

4. All our human insight fails as soon as we reach basic powers or faculties.

5. Rational nature is distinguished from the rest of nature by setting itself an end.

6. All men attribute freedom of will to themselves.

7. Have courage to use your own understanding.

8. Even if people were not compelled by internal dissent to submit to the coercion of public laws, war would produce the same effect from outside.

9. If a person cannot prove that a thing exists, he may attempt to prove that it does not exist.

10. A revolution may well put an end to autocratic despotism and to rapacious or self-seeking oppression, but it will never produce a true reform in ways of thinking.

Soren Kierkegaard

1. One must know oneself before knowing anything else.

2. One does not begin feasting at dawn but at sunset.

3. Genius, like a thunderstorm, comes up against the wind.

4. It requires moral courage to grieve; it requires religious courage to rejoice.

5. Boredom is the root of all evil, and it is this which must be kept at a distance.

6. The more you limit yourself, the more fertile you become in invention.

7. The eye with which you look at reality must constantly be changed.

8. Music finds its way where the rays of the sun cannot penetrate.

9. A man who cannot seduce men cannot save them either.

10. Children are always well-behaved as long as they are enjoying themselves.

Lao Tzu

1. Only when man recognizes beauty as such does ugliness become reality.

2. Who finds union of mind and heart will reach immortality.

3. Sincere words are not fine; fine words are not sincere.

4. There is no calamity greater than lightly engaging in war.

5. When the people do not fear what they ought to fear, that which is their great dread will be on them.

6. Who masters his passions and turns them to deeds of kindness, is greater than a king.

7. He who lightly promises is sure to keep but little faith.

8. He who knows other men is discerning; he who knows himself is intelligent.

9. No one can run with spread legs.

10. He who praises himself merits little appreciation.

John Locke

1. Things in print must stand and fall by their own worth, or the reader's fancy.

2. The candle that is set up in us shines bright enough for all our purposes.

3. Virtue and praise are so united that they are called often by the same name.

4. All that we desire is only to be happy.

5. Whoever reflects on what passes in his own mind cannot miss it.

6. The pictures drawn in our minds are laid in fading.

colors, and if not sometimes refreshed vanish and disappear.

7. A power to direct the operative faculties to motion or rest in particular instances is that which we call the will.

8. Men's principles, notions and relishes are so different, that it is hard to find a book which pleases or displeases all men.

9. Every step the mind takes in its progress toward knowledge makes some discovery, which is not only new, but the best too, for the time at least.

10. It is of great use to the sailor to know the length of his line, though he cannot with it fathom all the depths of the ocean.

Friedrich Wilhelm Nietzsche ─────────

1. Our treasure lies in the beehives of our knowledge.

2. Our thoughts should grow out of our values with the same necessity as the fruit out of the tree.

3. How blessed are we knowers, provided we know how to keep silent long enough!

4. It is a good thing that we do nothing for which we are not strong enough.

5. The poorer the memory of mankind has been, the more terrible have been its customs.

6. There is no feast without cruelty, as man's entire history attests.

7. All instincts that are not allowed free play turn inward.

8. There can be no doubt that bad conscience is a sickness, but so, in a sense, is pregnancy.

9. All good things have at one time been considered evil; every original sin has, at some point, turned into an original virtue.

10. All great things perish of their own accord, by an act of self-cancellation: so the law of life decrees.

Blaise Pascal

1. The whole visible world is but an imperceptible speck in the ample bosom of nature.

2. Benefits bestowed are welcome so long as they seem capable of repayment; after that gratitude turns to resentment.

3. Love and hate can change the face of justice.

4. No one speaks of us in our presence as in our absence.

5. Our very life depends on knowing whether the soul is mortal or immortal.

6. Man's greatness lies in his power of thought.

7. A man's worth is to be measured not by his spasmodic efforts but by his everyday life.

8. Human nature is not always advancing; it comes and goes.

9. Between us and hell or heaven there is only life, and that is the most fragile thing in the world.

10. The eternity of things in itself or in God must confound our brief duration.

Plato

1. It is good to have true beliefs, but bad to be in error.

2. Is it possible for someone who knows something not to know what he knows?

3. Each of us is the measure of the things that are and are not.

4. One can only believe what one is experiencing and this is always true.

5. Giving Socrates the opportunity for discussion is like giving cavalry the opportunity to fight on level ground.

6. No term can be meaningful without knowledge of what it stands for.

7. Man is the measure of all things—of the things that are, that they are; of the things that are not, that they are not.

8. Everything which we describe as 'being' is actually in the process of being generated as a result of movement and change and mutual mixture.

9. The process of generation—that is, apparent being—is a result of change: but destruction—that is, not being—is a result of inactivity.

10. There are two kinds of change, which may be distinguished not by their frequency of occurrence but by their powers: one is active, the other passive.

Will Rogers

1. Income tax has made more liars out of the American people than golf has.

2. A politician is not as narrow-minded as he forces himself to be.

3. My ancestors didn't come on the Mayflower but they met the boat.

4. I'd rather be right than Republican.

5. If your time is worth anything, travel by air. If not, you might just as well walk.

6. Swinging a rope is all right when your neck ain't in it.

7. Borrowing money on easy terms is a one-way ticket to the poorhouse.

8. Once a man holds a public office he is absolutely no good for honest work.

9. Any time a man can't come and settle with you without bringing his lawyer, why, look out for him.

10. America has never lost a war, or won a conference.

Bertrand Russell

1. Boredom as a factor in human behavior has received, in my opinion, far less attention than it deserves.

2. Every man would like to be God, if it were possible; some few find it difficult to admit the impossibility.

3. Rational apprehension of dangers is necessary; fear is not.

4. Instinct, mind and spirit are all essential to a full life; each has its own excellence and its own corruption.

5. No nation was ever so virtuous as each believes itself, and none was ever so wicked as each believes the other.

6. To save the world requires faith and courage; faith in reason, and courage to proclaim what reason shows to be true.

7. Sometimes, if pious men are to be believed, God's mercies are curiously selective.

8. Civic and personal morality are equally necessary to a good world.

9. Greed of possession will grow less when there is no fear of destitution.

10. Philosophers have only interpreted the world in various ways, but the real task is to alter it.

Jean-Paul Sartre

1. What distinguishes God from man is not greater freedom but greater power.

2. The very freedom to accept or reject the false is itself creative.

3. Sometimes the object of awareness will be something in the world, sometimes it will be the self.

4. Emotion is the transformation of the world.

5. What I ceaselessly aim towards is myself, that which I am not, my own possibilities.

6. Knowledge that other people exist, and are conscious, is part and parcel of our own awareness of ourselves.

7. It is the death of philosophy if it confuses the true with the convincing.

8. A free and conscious being cannot be possessed.

9. Nothing is superfluous if it is part of a rational plan.

10. Human actions must be divided into an inside and an outside—what a man intends, and what he does.

Arthur Schopenhauer

1. We have dreams; may not our whole life be a dream?

2. Life and dreams are leaves of the same book.

3. Nothing is to be had for gold but mediocrity.

4. While to the ordinary man his faculty of knowledge is a lamp to lighten his path, to a man of genius it is the sun which reveals the world.

5. Will is the thing-in-itself, the inner content, the essence of the world.

6. Life, the visible world, the phenomenon, is only the mirror of the will.

7. Time is like an unceasing stream, and the present a rock on which the stream breaks itself, but does not carry away with it.

8. Wrong which someone has inflicted upon me by no means entitles me to inflict wrong upon him.

9. Necessity is the kingdom of nature; freedom is the kingdom of grace.

10. With the exception of man, no being wonders at its own existence; but it is to them all so much a matter of course that they do not observe it.

Baruch Spinoza

1. Everything which is, is either in itself or in another.

2. The knowledge of an effect depends upon and involves the knowledge of the cause.

3. The will cannot be called a free cause, but can only be called necessary.

4. He who imagines that he affects others with joy or sorrow will necessarily be affected with joy or sorrow.

5. In every human mind some ideas are adequate, and others mutilated and confused.

6. The will and the intellect are one and the same.

7. Hatred is increased through return of hatred, but may be destroyed by love.

8. An emotion which is a passion ceases to be a passion as soon as we form a clear and distinct idea of it.

9. The human mind cannot be absolutely destroyed with the body, but something of it remains which is eternal.

10. The power of God is his essence itself.

Henry David Thoreau

1. It is not all books that are as dull as the readers.

2. The universe is wider than our view of it.

3. Heaven is under our feet as well as over our heads.

4. There is no odor so bad as that which arises from goodness tainted.

5. It is the luxurious and the dissipated who set the fashions which the herd so diligently follow.

6. To maintain one's self on this earth is not a hardship but a pastime if we live simply and wisely.

7. No face which we can give to a matter will stead us so well at last as the truth.

8. With respect to wit, I learned that there was not much difference between the half and the whole.

9. He who distinguishes the true savor of his food can never be a glutton; he who does not cannot be otherwise.

10. As every season seems best to us in its turn, so the coming in of spring is like the creation of cosmos out of chaos and the realization of the golden age.

Index